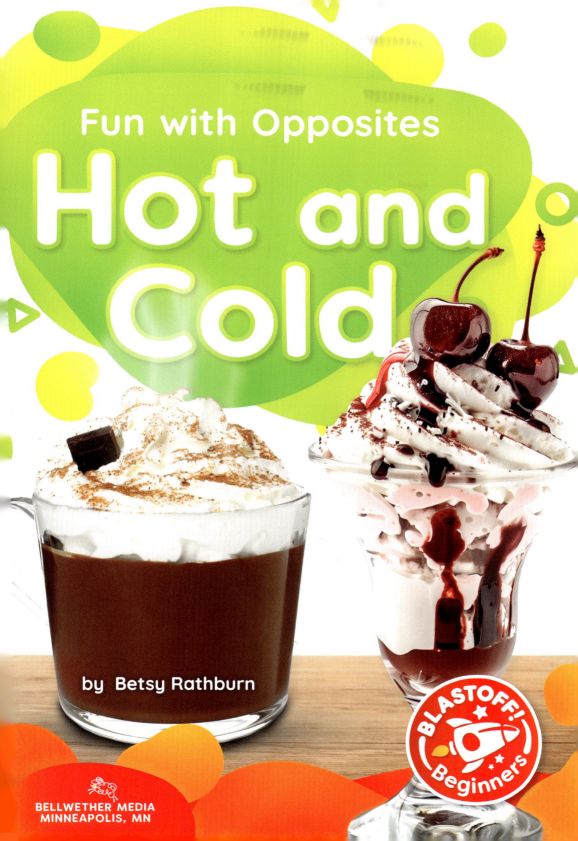

Fun with Opposites
Hot and Cold

by Betsy Rathburn

BELLWETHER MEDIA • MINNEAPOLIS, MN

BLASTOFF! Beginners

Blastoff! Beginners are developed by literacy experts and educators to meet the needs of early readers. These engaging informational texts support young children as they begin reading about their world. Through simple language and high frequency words paired with crisp, colorful photos, Blastoff! Beginners launch young readers into the universe of independent reading.

Sight Words in This Book 🔍

and	down	may	see	water
are	is	of	the	we
be	it	our	they	your
can	look	red	up	

This edition first published in 2026 by Bellwether Media, Inc.

No part of this publication may be reproduced in whole or in part without written permission of the publisher. For information regarding permission, write to Bellwether Media, Inc., Attention: Permissions Department, 3500 American Blvd W, Suite 150, Bloomington, MN 55431.

Library of Congress Cataloging-in-Publication Data

LC record for Hot and Cold available at: https://lccn.loc.gov/2025003233

Text copyright © 2026 by Bellwether Media, Inc. BLASTOFF! BEGINNERS and associated logos are trademarks and/or registered trademarks of Bellwether Media, Inc. Bellwether Media is a division of FlutterBee Education Group.

Editor: Rebecca Sabelko   Designer: Laura Sowers

Printed in the United States of America, North Mankato, MN.

Table of Contents

Beach Day	4
Two Opposites	6
Hot and Cold Things	12
Hot and Cold Facts	22
Glossary	23
To Learn More	24
Index	24

Beach Day

The sand is hot.
The cold water
cools us down!

Two Opposites

Hot and cold are **temperatures.**

Hot things
can look red.
They can burn!

Cold things may feel hard or dry. They can **freeze**!

Hot and Cold Things

Summer is hot.
Winter is cold.
We see our breath!

Deserts are often hot.
Mountains can be cold.

mountains

desert

Campfires are hot.
We cook.
Ice is cold.
We skate!

Hot drinks warm us up. Ice cream cools us down.

Think of your favorite food.
Is it hot or cold?

Hot and Cold Facts

Hot and Cold Around Us

cold snow

hot drink

Something Hot and Cold

summer

winter

Glossary

deserts

dry lands with few plants and little rainfall

freeze

to turn from water to ice

mountains

parts of land that rise higher than the land around it

temperatures

how hot or cold things are

To Learn More

ON THE WEB

FACTSURFER

Factsurfer.com gives you a safe, fun way to find more information.

1. Go to www.factsurfer.com.

2. Enter "hot and cold" into the search box and click 🔍.

3. Select your book cover to see a list of related content.

Index

burn, 8
campfires, 16
cook, 16
deserts, 14, 15
drinks, 18
food, 20
freeze, 10
ice, 16
ice cream, 18
mountains, 14
red, 8
sand, 4
skate, 16
summer, 12
temperatures, 6
water, 4
winter, 12

The images in this book are reproduced through the courtesy of: New Africa, front cover, p. 12; RubyLo, front cover; Tomas Ragina, p. 3; Ljupco Smokovski, p. 4; CandyRetriever, pp. 4-5; Marian Weyo, pp. 6-7 (thermometer); Evgeny Atamanenko, pp. 6-7; FotograFFF, p. 8; Carolyn Franks, pp. 8-9; Hurst Photo, p. 10; Standret, pp. 10-11; IURII KRASILNIKOV, pp. 12-13; Roman Babakin, p. 14; Dmitry Demkin, pp. 14-15; Dmytro Sheremeta, p. 16; ArtSvetlana, pp. 16-17; Matt Antonino, p. 18; LightField Studios, pp. 18-19; JeniFoto, pp. 20-21; Yuganov Konstantin, p. 22 (top); Juice Verve, p. 22 (summer); Olya Humeniuk, p. 22 (winter); Stefan Kostecki, p. 23 (deserts); Leonid Ikan, p. 23 (freeze); Capturas E, p. 23 (mountains); Mark van Dam, p. 23 (temperatures).